"REMEMBER: The Master Has Failed More Times Than The Beginner Has Even Tried"
- Stephen McCranie

BUILDING HABITS, SELF DISCIPLINE, AND CHARACTER THROUGH MARTIAL ARTS

MICHAEL HUANG

Copyright © 2024 Michael Huang

All rights reserved. No part of this book may be reprinted or reproduced or utilized in any form or by any electronic, mechanical, or other means, now known or hereafter invented, including photocopying and recording, or in information storage or retrieval systems, without permission in writing from the author.

The scanning, uploading and distribution of this book via the Internet or via any other means without the permission of the publisher is illegal and punishable by law.

Please purchase only authorized electronic editions and do not participate in or encourage electronic piracy of copyrighted materials. Your support of the author's rights is sincerely appreciated.

Printed in the United States of America.

First Printing: March 2023

"Remember: The Master Has Failed More Times Than The Beginner Has Even Tried."

~ Stephen McCranie

Dedication

A student recently gave my father and me a beautiful note with the following quote from polymath Albert Schweitzer.

"At times, our own light goes out and is rekindled by a spark from another person."

Each of us has cause to think with deep gratitude to those who have lit the flame within us.

My inspiration and goals would only be a dream without the support of those who believe in me. I want to take this opportunity to give thanks to the following people:

I am deeply grateful to my family for their unwavering support and for allowing me to pursue my passion for helping others through martial arts. My father has been a constant source of inspiration and learning for me. His unselfishness and the values he instilled in me, particularly the importance of giving, have shaped me into who I am today. I am truly grateful for his guidance.

My dreams and aspirations for relaying the torch are only meaningful because of the help from the Lifers and Inner Circle Group. Thank you for your unwavering support.

> "To laugh often and much; to win the respect of intelligent people and the affection of children; ... to appreciate beauty, to find the best in others; to leave the world a little better; whether by a healthy child or a garden patch ... to know even one life has breathed easier because you have lived. This is success."
>
> **Ralph Waldo Emerson**

Table of Contents

Chapter 1   Life Skills 1

Chapter 2   The World Is a Very Different Place 27

Chapter 3   Start with the End in Mind 33

Chapter 4   A Lesson from the Elephant 39

Chapter 5   It Starts with a Plan 45

Chapter 6   What's Next? 51

> *"The bigger the problem you can handle, the bigger the leader you can become."*
>
> ~ Grandmaster Huang, Chien-Liang

Chapter 1

Life Skills

If I had to summarize the reason I wrote this book, it would be to let parents know **with certainty** that if they give us 8 weeks with their child, they will see an undeniable change in their child's behavior, self-esteem, and work ethic.

Notice I didn't say they would be a world-class martial artist.

I didn't say they would win tournaments.

I didn't say they would break boards and do perfectly executed kicks.

In 8 weeks, you'll see the power of consistent effort and dedication. With the right guidance, a child who puts in the work, supported by involved parents who match our values, is unstoppable.

It's my belief that today's students need just as much (if not more) mental and emotional training – training they don't get in their regular school classroom or outside activities.

Yes, students can learn to:

- memorize the state capitals,
- throw a ball,
- or even run a faster 100-meter dash.

But most of the time, those things are just focused on specific skills.

They don't teach values, anti-bullying strategies, or how to build unshakable self-confidence while at the same time

www.uskuoshu.com

providing functional training and improving health and energy.

But I happen to think that building values and character is just as important, which is why I have spent years building a curriculum to bring out the very best in all our students.

You've probably heard of categorizing people as book smart or street smart. Many people seem to think you can only be one or the other and most have their opinions on which one is better.

Psychologists have said there are actually four types of intelligence:

1. Intelligence Quotient (IQ)

2. Emotional Quotient (EQ)

3. Social Quotient (SQ)

4. Adversity Quotient (AQ)

Call 443-394-9222 to get started

Your EQ represents your character while your SQ indicates your charisma. When faced with troubles, your AQ determines whether you can be a leader.

Most schools and parents emphasize improving IQ levels while the other areas aren't cultivated.

Being a parent has always been difficult, but now the prevalence and dependency on technology and social media make it challenging to raise a child with a variety of experiences that will help them face the world as an adult.

www.uskuoshu.com

Realities of Social Media

60 Minutes did a whole program about how much social media negatively impacts youth and adults.

The story is getting way too familiar:

> Parents give their children a cell phone with the idea that it'll keep them safe. Instead, the cell phone becomes the door into a dark world, even with parental controls.

60 Minutes shared that previously unpublished internal documents revealed that social media companies knew their platform was pushing kids to harmful content.

Parents are finally waking up, and more than 2,000 families are suing social media companies over kids' mental health.

> "The U.S. surgeon general has called it an 'urgent public health

crisis' — a devastating decline in the mental health of kids across the country. According to the CDC, the rates of suicide, self-harm, anxiety and depression are up among adolescents — a trend that began before the pandemic."

Kids, young people, and every adult need a safe place where discipline, community, and respect are stressed.

Where social media is not celebrated and encouraged.

Where real-life human, person-to-person caring, and discipline interaction is happening. Now more than ever, our school plays a vital role where people can re-center and find balance in their lives.

As a parent, do you find yourself struggling to help your child with any of the following scenarios?

1. Does your child have anxiety in a variety of situations or isn't reaching their full potential?

2. Does your child lack focus or have strong negative emotions (e.g., anger or depression)?

3. Does your child misbehave or lack discipline?

Perhaps they're lacking adversity in a safe environment, are in need of more physical activity, or are not empathizing with others and understanding how to show respect.

Dealing with adversity is inherent in martial arts where you need to learn and execute challenging techniques. **Failure is welcomed and encouraged at U.S. Kuo Shu Academy because we often learn more from our failures than our successes.**

Our school will not only challenge your child physically but also mentally because they need to focus on controlling their body. You'll find they leave class *smiling and re-energized* despite what may have happened earlier in their day.

USKSA is a community of teachers and students who help one another succeed. Your child will always receive respect and empathy from teachers during class, and your child may also provide support to another student who is struggling or having a bad day.

Respect is embedded in our school culture and it will become a habit for your child to show respect the more they receive it and give it.

A child who is committed to learning martial arts will most certainly increase their IQ, EQ, SQ, and AQ. They won't be known as only having book smarts or street smarts; they'll be known as having *life smarts*!

Why character (and life skills) are so important

Story of High Point University

I have a mentor who works directly with High Point University in North Carolina. High Point offers a range of courses that focus on developing practical life skills. These courses cover topics such as financial literacy, personal branding, communication skills, leadership development, and ethical decision-making. The aim is to equip students with the necessary skills to navigate various aspects of their personal and professional lives.

The reason they focus so much on life skills is because the president of the university, Nido Qubein, knows firsthand how important those skills are.

In fact, he teaches a class to all freshmen titled, "the President's Seminar on Life Skills."

Qubein came to the U.S. as a teenager with $50 in his pocket and little English and rose as an internationally known author, consultant, speaker, and entrepreneur. In 2005, he was asked to become president of High Point and use his business knowledge and skills to transform the university.

Key to the school's transformation has been the focus on not just technical training, but life-skills training.

In 2018 and again in 2022, Qubein and High Point University commissioned a survey to gain insight from executives across America on what it takes to succeed.

No matter what's happening in the world, executives ranked good character and life skills at the top for:

Getting a job.

Being successful on the job.

Getting a job promotion.

Unlike High Point, most colleges focus on the technical skills of a major, and almost all ignore basic life skills.

Here are the survey's results:

- Employers believe universities across the nation are over emphasizing technical skills over life skills (67% vs. 33%) and wish colleges would instill more life skills than technical skills (65% vs. 35%).

- 91% of employers believe that learning how to socialize outside of work is important. Employers are most concerned about hiring someone with a lack of emotional intelligence and people skills above all else (68%).

When executives were asked for the single most important reason someone can be successful not only in their current role but also in moving up the corporate ladder:

- 53%: Growth Mindset and strong work ethic
- 26%: Positive Attitude and working well with others
- And only 22%: Technical know how

When asked which attributes were likely to cause employees to be skipped for promotion:

- 46%: Don't receive feedback and constructive criticism well
- 36%: Don't know how to solve complex problems
- And only 18%: Lack technical know how

These kinds of skills are the reason why USKSA students go on and often become top executives.

USKSA is known as "The Premier Character Building and Life Skills Martial Arts School"

People often say they want to be successful — live the best that life has to offer.

But they don't realize that they confuse wishful thinking with focused discipline to achieve that success.

Helping students turn wishful thinking into confident, successful adults with highly developed life skills is what makes us unique.

I've seen student after student walk through our doors and succeed beyond their wildest imagination.

Why?

Because we have over 50 years of working with students to not only create elite athletes but also to turn on their God-given belief system and core values resulting in uncommon success stories.

> **EVERYONE MUST CHOOSE ONE OF TWO PAINS**
> — THE PAIN OF DISCIPLINE —
> OR THE PAIN OF REGRET
> - Jim Rohn

Learning Life Skills since the Age of 3½

I've spent my entire life involved with martial arts under the guidance of my father, Grandmaster Huang, Chien-Liang (黃乾量).

When your father is a world-class Grandmaster, daily life becomes ongoing lessons through a martial arts lens.

My father was born in Malaysia and began his martial arts training at the age of 12. By age 19, he had moved to Taiwan to attend the university and began studying with his Shi Ye, Supreme Master Wang, Chueh-Jen (王珏鑫). (For those unfamiliar with the term, "Shi Ye" is the traditional reference for a teacher of Northern Chinese martial arts.)

In 1972, he was invited to move to America and teach Kung Fu, and three years later, he had an opportunity to open his own Tien Sun Wushu school in Ohio while continuing his own training under his Shi Ye.

In his school, he focused on teaching a more traditional way of martial arts combined with the development of good character: respect, loyalty, humility, and compassion.

All success traits.

All ancient martial arts traits.

Since then, we have taught and promoted Chinese martial arts in over 30 countries and were ranked as one of the most impactful martial artists in the 20th century by *Inside Kung-Fu* because of our students' success and contribution in martial arts.

Our academy has been referred to as a *Maker of Champions and Builder of Character.*

Today, we have schools in Europe, the U.S., and South America.

My Early Years Post College

I started a different career path from my father, I went to college and graduated from the business school at the University of Maryland, landing a job right out of school with a high-end investment firm.

The most valuable thing I received from that job was being able to learn the mindset and thinking of one of the top investors in the country.

How he thought.

How he reacted.

How he looked at the pros and cons of anything he was doing.

It was a great learning environment, but when my hours kept getting longer and longer, and having gained 50 pounds, I knew it was time to return to my martial arts roots.

This was not the easy path to take and a lot of sacrifices had to be made. Success on the mat doesn't always translate into business success.

When I first decided to make martial arts my full-time job, the school could only afford to pay me $300 a month. I couldn't even earn enough to pay for my cost of living.

I used all of my savings to keep myself going and **do something I believed in.** To ensure multiple schools could be open for students, I never paid myself *anything* for more than eight years.

If you were to ask any school owner if they could teach martial arts full-time, they would likely express their enthusiasm for such an opportunity.

I feel very fortunate to be in this position, which wouldn't have been possible without the life skills I've acquired.

I want to give others the same ability to pursue their passion, which I can tell you will be difficult and require perseverance.

That's why I've taken the lessons I learned from the master investor and implemented them into our elite martial arts school.

It is the best of both worlds.

Top mindset combined with Chinese martial arts!

Martial arts is not a hobby for me — it's a way of life, and that is why our school is anything but ordinary.

You can get ordinary at the local community center or a rented gym.

Here we teach — and expect — all our students to not only grow physically as they learn traditional Chinese Kung Fu (Kuo Shu), we also focus on developing the students' minds, bodies, and spirits to set them on a course for life-long success.

We fill the gaps children don't get in their academic school classroom or after-school sports.

It took me nearly 20 years to develop the character values and lessons we teach.

That's two decades of doing mat lessons (also called mat chats) week after week, and fine tuning until we're known internationally as developing elite students.

Many people have the idea that martial artists are under-educated and have no other options. They would be wrong.

Especially at our school, many top executives, professionals, and leaders seek martial arts training. Why? Because even if you have all the money in the world, there is no better investment than investing in yourself. No amount of money can buy health and skill; you have to train, and train with the best.

These days I focus primarily on the advanced students, but I am always careful to see how the younger students are doing under the guidance of my well-trained instructors.

This is not the easy button.

I will be upfront with you.

What I teach in our martial arts school is not easy.

Your child will be tested both physically and mentally.

If you're looking for the easy button or just a babysitting place, you should probably close this book and move on. I'm not for you.

The Family Is Just As Important

When we evaluate our students, we also look at their family. The parent(s) must be involved with their child and share our values of respect and discipline.

Some days it may be tough to get your child to come to class. I can't go to your house, knock on your door, and pull them away from what they're doing. Only you can do that by setting clear and consistent expectations.

But I can guarantee that your child will have a great time in class and that every 8 weeks, you'll see the growth and development of your child in a demonstration of their techniques.

If you are looking for a life-changing, life-altering experience, and training for your child — and match our values — then I respectfully encourage you to take the 30 minutes it will take to read this book.

I kept it short on purpose.

You can't really know how your child will grow and change until they come week after week and you watch the growth and change.

You may never have thought of enrolling your child at a martial arts academy…**but what if it was THE key to their best achievement?**

See for yourself and read the testimonials from students and parents throughout this book and on our website at www.USKuoShu.com.

These stories have been passed down by my father and then through me over the 50 years of our students living successful lives.

Thank you for taking the 30-minute journey with me to read this book. I'm hoping in the end, you'll agree that it makes sense to schedule a free Evaluation Lesson.

Let's get started!

Master Michael Huang

www.uskuoshu.com

"A school that focuses on character development."

I love this Academy for my son.

His development has been amazing with his focus, confidence, and communication.

The teachers are so patient, knowledgeable, and skillful.

If you want a school that focuses on character development and being a good person along with setting personal goals...This is the place for you and your family!!!!!!!

Tanesha Collins

SEVEN WORDS OF RESPECT

Yes Sir

Yes Ma'am

No Sir

No Ma'am

Thank You

You're Welcome

Please

Chapter 2

The World Is a Very Different Place

"Kids these days!"

That's a comment many people use to suggest kids are lazy, entitled, disrespectful, demanding, and defiant.

Just like you, I've seen those kids in restaurants, in sporting events, and in everyday activities.

The feeling is that kids these days are somehow different from other generations.

I disagree that kids are different.

But what I do agree with is that they are living in a much different environment than past generations, with far more opportunities to go down the wrong path.

When parents send their children off to school, they are not only concerned about their well-being but also about what they'll have to deal with in school and out of school.

71% of parents admitted that their worry intensifies when their child starts their first day of classes.

Here are some statistics to put these things into perspective:

1. The rate of aggravated assaults in the U.S. went from 50 per 100,000 in 1957 to 284 per 100,000 in 2021.

2. According to John Hopkins Medicine, as children grow and develop, they can be easily influenced by what they see and hear, especially on television — and

now social media. Too much screen time can lead to obesity, sleep problems, depression, anxiety, and lower standardized test scores. Today, not only do children have television to watch, but often carry around phones that keep them distracted 24/7.

3. According to the Department of Justice:

   a. Children exposed to violence are more likely to abuse drugs and alcohol; suffer from depression, anxiety, and post-traumatic disorders; fail or have difficulty in school; and become delinquent and engage in criminal behavior.

   b. 60% of American children were exposed to violence, crime, or abuse in their homes, schools, and communities.

    c. Almost 40% of American children were direct victims of two or more violent acts, and 1-in-10 were victims of violence five or more times.

    d. Children are more likely to be exposed to violence and crime than adults.

    e. The massive media exposure of sex and violence is taking a huge toll on our children and our society as a whole.

4. Bullying has become an epidemic in our schools, and it's taking a devastating toll on our teens.

    a. 1-in-3 students report being bullied.

    b. 62% of students who reported being bullied said it occurred at school.

c. Students who experience bullying are at increased risk for suicide.

d. Nearly 1 in 5 students who reported being bullied seriously considered suicide.

e. Suicide rates among teens have been on the rise in recent years.

Parents these days are feeling overwhelmed trying to guide and protect their children.

They are looking for ways to help their children grow up well-adjusted, happy, and successful.

Value-Based Martial Arts

This is why my value-based, character development martial arts curriculum becomes so important.

In the next chapter, I'm going to share the #1 reason why our students are so successful in life.

> "You will find no ego or bravado here, just positivity, discipline, and inspiration to become the best possible version of yourself."

I have had the privilege of learning from Grandmaster Huang over the last 20 years when he comes to visit our school to teach seminars every year. He is a true martial artist in the traditional sense — discipline, wisdom, and respect are foundational pillars of his character, but I have also always appreciated his sense of humor.

Ann Jae
Three-time World Champion in form and full-contact fighting

Chapter 3

Start with the End in Mind

It was Stephen Covey in his book, *Seven Principles of Highly Effective People,* who said,

"Always start with the end in mind."

I agree.

This is why whenever new students start with us, we focus on the end goal: **Black Sash**.

You might have heard of martial arts schools using colored ranking belts, with a black belt being the highest. In our school, we use sashes, but the concepts are the same.

Everything we do is focused on the psychology of achieving the top prize (e.g., the black sash).

To earn a black sash, students must apply the mental and emotional skills of:

- Short- and long-term goal setting.
- Creating habits of focus, discipline, and follow through.
- Overcoming negative peer pressure.

These skills must be learned and demonstrated, both in and out of class, before a student earns a Black Sash.

www.uskuoshu.com

You will often hear me say "WE ARE A BLACK SASH SCHOOL!"

When a child comes for the first time, they start with an Evaluation Lesson.

The purpose of our Evaluation Lesson is to prepare a student to set a goal to BLACK SASH & BEYOND!

- Your child's instructors will be looking to see *if they qualify for U.S. Kuo Shu Academy's Black Sash Leadership Program.*

- This process can take AS LITTLE as 4-8 weeks. However, it may take longer, depending on the dedication and attitude shown by the student and how supportive their family is in their training.

- A student is invited to continue into Black Sash Leadership only if they show us they are serious about applying the Black Sash habits and attitudes they learn in class.

It's the #1 reason our students excel in life and their careers.

They're expected to break through limiting beliefs and excel!!! And they do.

We are a "No Excuses" school.

The purpose of the Evaluation Lesson is to give prospective students an overview of the school. From there, the student's main objective is to qualify for our Black Sash Leadership Program.

DEVELOPMENT RATE BY PROGRAM

BLACK SASH LEADERSHIP

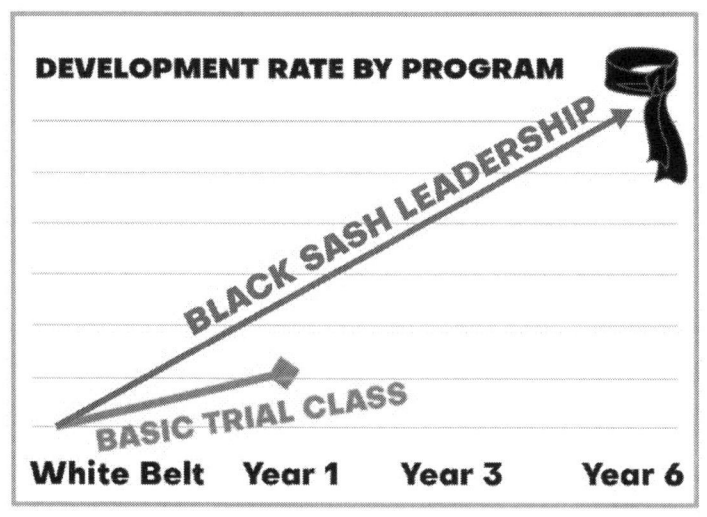

BASIC TRIAL CLASS

White Belt — Year 1 — Year 3 — Year 6

It doesn't even matter if the student has attention problems or disabilities.

If the parent(s) are committed to supporting our value-based curriculum, we welcome **all** students.

In the next chapter, I'm going to share the biggest lesson our students must first learn.

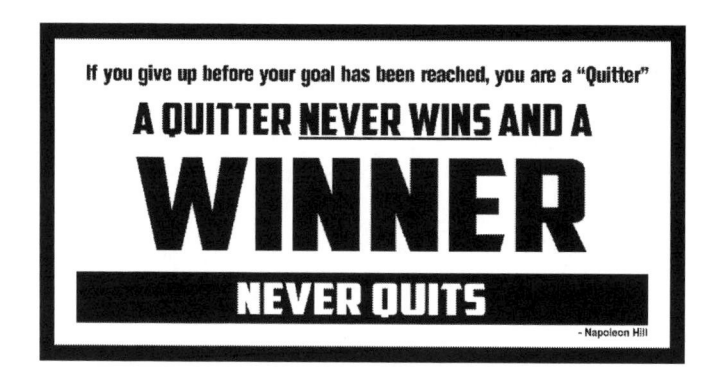

> If you give up before your goal has been reached, you are a "Quitter"
>
> **A QUITTER NEVER WINS AND A WINNER NEVER QUITS**
>
> - Napoleon Hill

"We highly recommend U.S. Kuo Shu Academy to students of all ages."

My children and I have been privileged and honored to train with Grandmaster Huang for many years through numerous seminars. The opportunity to train with him is INVALUABLE given his wealth of KNOWLEDGE and DEDICATION in traditional Chinese martial arts, focusing on mind, body & spirit. We have known Grandmaster Huang, Master Michael Huang, and their instructor staff for more than 14 years, and we hold them in the highest regard. Their dedication to martial arts and their students is exceptional. We highly recommend U.S. Kuo Shu Academy to students of all ages who are interested in authentic and high-quality martial arts training for themselves and/or their family members.

Janice Fitzsimmons
Bok Fu Do Black Belt

Chapter 4

A Lesson from the Elephant

Elephants are one of the largest and most powerful creatures on earth. They could crush anything or anyone in their way, but when you go to the zoo or circus, you see them sitting quietly held only by a small chain or rope.

How is this possible?

Because of "elephant chaining."

When an elephant is a baby, they are tied down with chains (or ropes) that are too strong for them to break through.

They will struggle and try, but they can never break the chain and get free.

As they try, the chain will tear into their skin causing pain. The pain causes them to stop trying.

As they grow, their trainers can use smaller and smaller chains to hold them, and they eventually will never try to break free again.

No matter how weak the chain or rope is, the elephant will not try to break it.

It's a lesson for every one of us.

From a very young age we are told NO and trained to avoid trying to do the "impossible."

Why don't we:

- Try out for a class play?
- Study hard to get the top grade on a test?
- Apply for that job?
- Ask that special person on a date?

It's because somewhere in the past we were chained to the belief that we couldn't do it, weren't good enough, or we got burned once trying.

We gave up because, "Why try the impossible?"

We slip into a pattern of only trying things we perceive as easy and achievable. We never stretch and simply accept a life of mediocrity.

This is why our Black Sash martial arts training is life-changing for students.

We focus on what Carol Dweck (Author of *Growth Mindset* and professor of psychology at Stanford University) refers to as a "growth mindset." A mindset where abilities are not set in stone.

We challenge students to get past their fears and insecurities and realize they can do the impossible.

I once read a story of a teacher who told a group of students they had above-average intelligence and was going to be moved into an advanced class.

They were told they were highly gifted and special.

In reality, they just tested average, but they didn't know it.

If they knew they were average, they could have had excuses like:

- "The work will be too hard."
- "I'm not smart enough."
- "There's no way I can make it in that class."

But because they were told they were above average, they all excelled.

In fact, ALL of them ended up with A's and B's.

It was simply an issue of their belief — never an issue of their intelligence.

A chained (or fixed) mindset can be the biggest obstacle to lifelong success.

We teach our Black Sash students the benefits of tugging on that chain and breaking through.

The only way they fail is by not trying.

It all starts with a plan.

> ## "The instructors are all top notch, professional and truly care about each and every student."
>
> *My son and I are both students at USKSA and it has been an awesome experience for us. I've really enjoyed watching my son DEVELOP DISCIPLINE and RESPECT while learning the fundamentals of Tien Shan Pai. The instructors are all top-notch, professional and truly care about each and every student. In addition to learning Kung Fu, my flexibility, endurance and coordination have all greatly improved. I'm very pleased with my experience and would recommend USKSA to anyone!*
>
> **Ray Ro**

Chapter 5

It Starts with a Plan

Hopefully, by now, you can see that our school is not your ordinary martial arts school.

Yes, we train elite athletes, but more than that, we train students to be well-adjusted, successful adults.

A Plan for Success Starts with the First Lesson

Here we teach — and expect — all our students to not only grow physically as they learn traditional Chinese Kung Fu (Kuo Shu). We also focus on developing the students' minds, bodies, and spirits to set them on a course for life-long success.

Everything we do is planned and scheduled. It starts on day one.

Each week the young students get assignments with expectations.

It starts with memorizing their schedule.

MY KUNG FU SCHEDULE

STEP 1: MEMORIZE YOUR SCHEDULE
A BLACK SASH takes responsibility for their training and ensures they make time for it. One of your primary tasks as a student is to memorize your class schedule and create a consistent training schedule at home. This will help you anchor in good habits and get the most out of your training.

DAY	START TIME	END TIME

www.uskuoshu.com

Setting goals

STEP 2: SET GOALS FOR YOUR NEXT SASH ... AND BEYOND!
A BLACK SASH always thinks about the next step toward their goal. What skills and techniques must you be proficient in before you can advance to your next sash? A way to reach your goal is by starting at the end and working your way backward.

1. "I will earn my 2nd degree Black Sash in _____ (month) _____ (year)."
2. "I will earn my 1st degree Black Sash in _____ (month) _____ (year)."
3. "My next Promotion Ceremony is ____ weeks away on _____ (month) _____ (day)."
4. "My Sash Evaluation (testing) starts on _____."
5. "My next Progress Check will be on _____ (date)."
6. "Before I can start my Sash Evaluation, I will need to attend _____ classes and complete _____ character development stripes."

The sooner you're able to create the right habits and discipline yourself, the easier being successful and a leader will become -- not only at the school, but in your community!

My Next Rank	

Memorizing the creed

STEP 3: MEMORIZE THE CREEDS
A BLACK SASH strives to live by the USKSA STUDENT and TIEN SHAN PAI creeds. This means never being abusive in any way, and always showing a positive attitude toward family, friends, peers, and instructors.

USKSA Student Creed	Tien Shan Pai Creed
• I will develop myself physically, mentally, and emotionally based on the Tien Shan Pai motto. • I will only use my kung fu as a last resort. • I will do the best I can by not making excuses. • I will be honest and compassionate to myself and others. • I will earn my black sash.	Kuo Shu begins and ends with respect. As a dedicated Tien Shan Pai student, I will live by the motto and principles of a Tien Shan Pai black sash. Respect • Loyalty • Righteousness • Compassion

And scheduling progress checks with their instructor

STEP 4: PROGRESS CHECKS AND PRIVATE LESSONS
Your private instructor will schedule time to meet with you, or you and your family periodically to go over your progress in and out of class. For students under 17, both parents / all caregivers are required to attend. Be sure to stay in touch with your private instructor regularly.

Call 443-394-9222 to get started

The lessons are planned out week after week. Nothing is left to chance.

We call it the "Black Sash Leadership Plan."

"I am proud to be a part of the Kuo Shu family."

As a student of USKSA, I am proud to be a part of the Kuo Shu family. Everyone is treated with RESPECT and the instructors take their time to get to know their students.

When I started 3 years ago, I was very shy and quiet. My parents wanted me to learn Kung Fu so that if I ever encountered a dangerous situation I would be able to defend myself. As I continued my classes, I made new FRIENDS, learned new skills and gained more self confidence.

Now, I am a more outgoing person and I feel CONFIDENT that I can protect myself. I am proud to be a part of the Kuo Shu family.

Marina Leon

"Reaping the benefits of USKSA's teachings every day."

My Kung Fu journey began at this school when I was a toddler watching my older brother take classes and compete in tournaments. I used to stand in the lobby trying to follow along with the Kung Fu moves until I was old enough to start lessons myself.

Flash forward over twelve years, and I am now a college student reaping the benefits of U.S. Kuo Shu Academy's teachings EVERY DAY. U.S. Kuo Shu Academy is a place where everyone can feel welcome, find support, and grow to be the best version of themselves. When my U.S. Kuo Shu Academy journey began as a young child, I did not understand the extent to which Kung Fu would shape my life. I grew up at U.S. Kuo Shu Academy not just learning martial arts techniques and having fun (which you have lots of!) but also learning LIFE SKILLS that apply to all aspects of my life.

Margot Jay
Tien Shan Pai Black Sash
Engineering Student at Washington University

Chapter 6

What's Next?

First, I'd like to thank you for reading this short book.

I purposely kept it short. I could continue to tell you about our history, why we're different, and the benefits of enrolling in our Evaluation Lesson. However, until you and your child

- actually experience it,
- watch us in action,
- see what we require of you,

you won't truly know the reason why we are an elite school that is trusted by high-profile students.

www.uskuoshu.com

This is why I have a "Prove It to Me, Michael" offer.

Call my school at 443-394-9222 and tell us you'd like your child to come to an Evaluation Lesson.

We'll get them scheduled.

No Risk to You!!

I'm going to take all the risk and invite your child to come *for free* the first time to see if we'll be a good fit. (No... I don't accept everyone who wants to join our Black Sash program.)

You, as the parent(s), must match our values, and your child must be committed to their weekly assignments.

Give us a call at 443-394-9222 and let's get your child started.

I'm honored to work with every child that parents entrust us to teach

www.uskuoshu.com

character values while at the same time teaching martial arts disciplines.

I'm looking forward to seeing your child's name on the class schedule.

Master Michael Huang

★ ★ ★ ★ ★

"One of the finest Chinese Martial Arts schools in the country."

Nelson Ferriera
Master Instructor for Zhong Yi Kung Fu Association

One of the finest Chinese martial arts schools in the country. Some of the best competitors and teachers that I've ever met come from this fine school. It has a tradition of excellence in all they do. Grandmaster Huang, Chien-Liang and the US Kuo Shu Academy build champions with integrity.

www.uskuoshu.com

⭐⭐⭐⭐⭐

"The Best School of Martial Arts"

Irvin Lee
Parent of two at U.S. Kuo Shu Academy

My children have been students for more than 4 years now and they love this school of martial arts. US Kuo Shu Academy is their second home, learning not just kung fu but also developing one's character as a good, responsible, respectful and disciplined citizen. Thank you very much Grandmaster Huang, Master Michael Huang and all the teachers and studetns for making this place the best school of martial arts.

★ ★ ★ ★ ★

"They learn many ways of defending themselves, gaining self-confidence and improve many aspects of their well-being."

Mark Babasa
Parent of four at U.S. Kuo Shu Academy

We have 2 kids who have taken kung fu here for nearly 3 years and they have benefited tremendously from it. They learn many ways of defending themselves, gain self-confience and improve many apsects of their physical well-being (strength, flexibility, etc.) and learn discipline and self-motivation. The school has many world-champion instructors and a very well-thought-out curriculum.

www.uskuoshu.com

★ ★ ★ ★ ★

"What I learn here directly translates to how I approach every challenge I've had with school or otherwise."

Mitchell Jay
Graduate of Yale University and Beth Tfiloh Congregation & Community School

I started taking lessons at US Kuo Shu Academy when I was five years old. Each aspect of my USKSA training has helped me navigate ... challenges inside and outside of martial arts. I can attribute nearly all of my achievements, from earning my black sash and competing in Lei Tai to graduating college and applying to medical school, to the USKSA. Each goal has built on itself and helped me with the other, creating a large web of goals that are intimately related and cannot be separated; every opportunity to teach, push myself, and realize my potential in Kung Fu has also helped me maintain self-confidence outside of martial arts. There is no better investment for your physical mental and emotional well-being.

Call 443-394-9222 to get started

If you're not ready to take the next step, watch our "ABOUT US" video on YouTube to learn more.

Made in the USA
Middletown, DE
24 August 2024